Praise for *I Remember Death*
by Its Proximity to What I Love

"I have never read a book quite like *I Remember Death by Its Proximity to What I Love*, which explores a daughter's longing for her father—a persistent and haunting spirit. There are endless pathways to read this searingly intelligent collection, full of magical footnotes, journalistic asides, and love notes to readers as it measures abiding love against societal threat, as it weighs personal loss against national gain. I praise Mahogany L. Browne, who is a fire starter, a conjurer of essential prayer, and a torchbearer who lights the way to justice. Her words are flames, igniting love and its essential truth. This book is an act of supreme invention that wills itself to survive through powerful insistence."

—TINA CHANG, Brooklyn Poet Laureate, author of *Hybrida*

"Because we work so hard to deny our vulnerability—to those we love, to those who love us, and to those whom we know mean us harm—we often find ourselves on edge, hoping no one will see that we're afraid, that we're breakable. In this intimate, book-length poetic journey, Mahogany L. Browne carefully examines vulnerability in herself, in her family, and, by extension, the fragility of all Black Americans who find ourselves living in a nation that often does not love us. It is the raw honesty with which Ms. Browne dissects this painful position that breaks the spell and offers a way out of the psychosis induced by a country that remains unwilling to take on its own history. This book is not an elaborate complaint; it is a crack in the wall of despair."

—TIM SEIBLES, Virginia Poet Laureate, author of *Hurdy Gurdy*

"Mahogany L. Browne is the geometer and keeper of our sacred realities; Thelonious Monk casually playing a crossroad blues. In this collection of poems, she raises even the heirlooms of the dead; every molecule of a path home. A leap into revolution. Telling our whole lives. Here on paper are the mannerisms of a hurricane; like looking at a poem and seeing that your big sister is God."

—TONGO EISEN-MARTIN, San Francisco Poet Laureate, author of *Heaven Is All Goodbyes*

I REMEMBER DEATH
BY ITS PROXIMITY
TO WHAT I LOVE

Mahogany L. Browne

Haymarket Books
Chicago, Illinois

Published in 2021 by
Haymarket Books
P.O. Box 180165
Chicago, IL 60618
773-583-7884
www.haymarketbooks.org
info@haymarketbooks.org

ISBN: 978-1-64259-570-3

Distributed to the trade in the US through Consortium Book Sales
and Distribution (www.cbsd.com) and internationally through Ingram
Publisher Services International (www.ingramcontent.com).

This book was published with the generous support of Lannan Foun-
dation and Wallace Action Fund.

Special discounts are available for bulk purchases by organizations
and institutions. Please email info@haymarketbooks.org for more
information.

Cover artwork Patrick Dougher.
Cover design by Julie Fain.

Printed in Canada by union labor.

Library of Congress Cataloging-in-Publication data is available.

10 9 8 7 6 5 4 3 2 1

Table of Contents

Part I

If my mother were ever convicted for her addiction
like my father
I wonder who I would be robbing now

The data from the Fragile Families Study says
My kind of survival displays more behavioral problems
and early juvenile delinquency
I say, *You right*

I rode the night with a pistol in my gray hoodie
—spitting image of my father
His nickname akin to boom
His red skin the only thing I remember
Him towering over me
Black hair red bloodshot eyes
Already running
Already gone

This was the closest time I ever came to becoming
a woman with a number for a name

It is easier than you think
to lose yourself in search
of resemblance

       Politicians with expensive silk ties
       cut taxes
       pad pockets
       sterilize would-be mothers

2

charge their district with the bill
Cue reality TV series

Suggest art programs to settle the inmates
& wonder why humans climb the walls
trying to escape their own skin
after the teaching artist
is asked to stop
bringing poems
that encourage
Collective behavior

A) father gifts you his hands
2) your mother laughs w/ the breath of a ghost C) no one remembers how much you cried 5) there are more houses in your throat than you can count E) you forgot how to count because you forget how to say *i love you* 8) your grandmother is a steeple 9) you love how love sounds more than you know how it works 10) you love how love works more than you know how to hold the pieces 11) your father showed you how love works with his absent mouth J) i love you K) your grandmother is a steeple—you are only a cemetery meandering 14) you can bury anything inside these hands 14.5) you are best w/ dirt 15) you wear a printed t-shirt to the local farmer's market—the blk letters read: do not get lost here, there is nothing but white soot

Marathon runs of *Wentworth*

mist the room like smoke clouds
I know TV is only TV to someone
that ain't never been forced to look
outside their own heartbreak before[1]

What's a cliff dive to a Black man
hustled by his own country?

He earns 92 cents an hour
and my tuition still ain't free
The woman behind the financial aid counter
asks me what my father makes

I say

                    Furniture for the dorms here

I say

                    Grand fatherless children

I say

---

[1] I binge-watch the Australian television drama. After a several-week
    streaming stint I find myself crying, crying, crying for the world
    which held my father and uncles and brother and cousins like a fist.

I don't know

I don't know

I don't know

who he is

No one prays for the babies

I enter the gates of a boy's prison
menacing the border of Bristol, England

    The smell that refuses to leave
    my jean jacket three days later
    must resemble the air of Pelican Bay

    I toss the jacket in the trash

    Privileged with the ability to push away
    the dilemma of a nation-induced disorder[2]

This must be the scent of apathy

    This is the closest I'll ever come
    to visiting my father

---

[2] "Nation Induced-Disorder" was the original name of this poem until
I realized it is a worldwide condition fueled by capitalism. This glob-
al epidemic is rampant in Thailand, Australia, Mexico, Honduras,
Brazil, Papua New Guinea, Ukraine, and Belize.

I remember death by its proximity to what I love the most

Yesterday
Nipsey Hussle was mowed down

in front of his clothing store
on Slauson and Crenshaw

The world raged, a forest of dying

like: a glaring of fangs brimming

into neighboring fur or a gang of buffalo
broadside beneath the Compton skyline or

a parade of elephant eulogies moving in silence

or a cauldron of bats darkening every street to
match the *ardere* of a people

Our young
a romp of otter-uttered blessings facing

the bleak-faced crash as an ambush of
tigers scowl at their audacity

the babies wail for justice
their screams full of drift and red blues

This is how we grieve:

candles and teddy bears and flowers and posters
tears and prayer hands and wailing and wailing
fighting and swinging and singing and sanging
for the flawed men that search for redemption

for men that remind us of home

Just minutes away in Inglewood, California,
my uncle pulls his blue plastic folding chair
under the nearest shaded tree in the communal yard
to watch the passersby

My uncle's youngest brother's been dead for years
He sits outside anyway
I wonder if he can still smell
the See's Candies factory two blocks away

    Does he remember
    how sweet and satisfying it taste
    after we pooled our mangled silver
    together for lollipops?

    Does he still wait for my gone uncle to visit?

    Is that what he's risking under the sun?

I remember death

When my favorite cousin, Andrew, is murdered, a shotgun blast to the dome, I am in Sacramento, preparing for my little league softball finals. I play my position(s): catcher or third base. I want to be a pitcher. I want to deliver the strikeouts. But the daughter of the coach is much more consistent than I am. So, I play my position(s). I guard where I'm told. I never tag anyone out. We don't win the season. I decide I love the game even if I never win. I decide I love the game even if it never loves me back.

I remember

When I return home, my mother is nowhere to be seen. But her smell is everywhere. I don't burden her with the bad news. Her child didn't win. But when I hear a gasp somewhere behind her closed door, I figure she knows what I know. I don't think twice of the phone's plastic echo as it returns to its cradle in haste::

Andrew, a teenager with a brilliant smile:: Andrew, just out of jail:: Andrew, my favorite cousin:: Andrew, could erupt a room into the confetti of joy:: Andrew, a gunshot wound to the head:: Andrew, bloody and dying in front of our cousin who screamed and cried and cradled his face in one hand / her other hand holding close her newborn son:: When I hear her name at our family barbecue years later, after she's testified against the killers and lost her spirit to dance with friends:: I make her a new world

I decide she must
look like she's never held
a dead boy before

Her mushroom hairstyle
is asymmetric and perfect
Her eyes shine
Maybe she still smiles and drinks
her sweet Pepsi

So
if I can write
I do
if I can write
I do

I remember death

Today, when the sky is forgiving enough
and the smog pretends itself an heirloom of history
I am sky dumb-cloud sick until still
There
in the corner of my smile
                is a poem waiting to be picked up
dusted off
and shined real good

But all I can muster
is the strength to pull myself

                to the bathroom mirror
and try to (re)locate my father's rage

Instead I find you

silly poem

waiting to be seen

waiting to be

If I can write
I do
if I can write
I do
I can write
I do

I remember death by its proximity to what I love

The quietest time of the day

is when I hold my breath

sit back and suck in my stomach

close my eyes into thin slits

and whistle

The room is only a room
not judge and jury
not a system of impossible fractions

When I share this poem

shape the aftermath of a mudslide

into something compact

and ready to be carried into the world

beyond the steel bars

I pretend my father is in the back of the room

Red Red Baby[3]

His nickname

go

---

[3] Of course, you want to know what my father must have done to be locked up all my life. How many drugs did he sell? How many bodies did he leave without breath? None. None, of course, dear reader. You cannot imagine a thief so spectacular, so magical in his sleight of hand, that he left the world without a trace. Or manslaughter? Or abuse? Or addiction? Of course. Of course. All of the above? Possibly a collage of victimless crimes? No, just the audacity to refuse a plea. Mercy.

I wonder:[4]

Does he approve
of my line breaks?

How strategic I can be
as I pass his carcass throughout
the audience like an offering

---

[4] As I am writing this in a time in which poets accuse each other of
noncommittal words (like "wonder"), if I may interject: this placement
of the word simply acknowledges that that writer / narrator is still
in search of an answer to the wonderment presented. But, lean in,
friend, let me tell you what I know: the writer's father has been gone,
gone, gone, and so, she fears she will never truly understand or know.
Yes, this moment of unknowing is her attempt to completely level
the obstructed field of vision. It is ultimately an example of how the
writer imagines her father, whole. And how the writer deconstructs
the intention behind these daughter-sans-daddy-induced theories.

28

I give till gone
till dust
till smoke

An abandoned child
works harder for a longer gaze

a position closest to the sun

I remember death by its proximity to what I love the most.
And the most never looks like freedom, not really.

A song on repeat:
you're my favorite

you're my heart

you're mine

you're mine

The lover you learn to love
will never understand

Why you cry?
Why you wait up late at night?
Why you double-check the rearview mirror?

Why you cry
Why you worry about who
and what got the loyalty
to carry your name

Why you cry and rock
yourself into a corner of yourself
Why you walk through the world

dry faced
pursed lips
eyes cold

The internally weeping
collect their own ghosts

Your lover wants to love you in return
but will begin to understand
your kind of love requires
a space for constant grieving

Ain't no man ya DADDY
    Sleep w/ a broken bulb above the porch
    listen carefully for the haunt the b o n e s h a t t e r
      listen as it shuffles across threshold
a blue & gluttonous rat

Ain't NO man ya daddy
      Find a man w/ soft eyes Find a man
      w/ no hands Find a man w/ no home
            PRAY

Ain't no MAN ya daddy
         When the first moon spills open like
a cavernous beast & your
mother forgets to draw the curtains
of her smile
     the floorboards can   be the sledgehammer
     flush a splinter from the base
beneath your big toe
     hold it like a pitchfork (or a gun)
         swing   (aim)
                boom

And in 2018, Crime Report[5] says
within three years of release,
about two-thirds (67.8 percent)
of released prisoners
will be rearrested.

---

[5] Crime Report is a study available free of charge through a nonprofit
program operating within the Center on Media Crime and Justice at
John Jay College in New York. This networking resource served as
a beacon when researching the archives of poet, warrior, and writer,
Audre Lorde. Lorde, like me, taught at John Jay College and was a
mother. Once, my own mother asked me why I was so angry. I was
in my early twenties and explosive when speaking about my father.
Lorde's work gave me the compass to redirect my anger.

I remember death by its proximity to what I love the most. And the most never looks like freedom, not really. So perfect bow and complete. But the argument of Freedom is not as clean as the driven snow. Not pure. There is blood and history there. Freedom is a container of blood and a living document. It is unanswered question. Remarkable position of positioning. Evergreen in the chase towards its promise. Unchanging coordinates. Accessible to barren land. Prison lacks the imagination. It is the constant undoing of our humanity. Atrophic muscle. Where freedom is a hopeful star. Dream of a memory so close the long whisp of a forgotten breath. Steel bars of unease // consistent qualms // mounting absent. I remember death by its proximity to what I love because incarceration promises everyone it touches: *you will not be the same.* Twenty-two years of prison is an off-balance of a dance towards your humanity. Away from true living. Uncertain chaos. Destruction of filament and family. Life and love are sometimes synonymous, sometimes not.

Prisoners

released

Two-thirds

rearrested

says

study[6]

---

[6] these fractures. Study these fractures. These fractures have been repurposed. Intentional rage. Intentional in recognizing the loss of my father. Intentional in naming the taking of blood. This system is blood hungry. Read the reports. The data will consistently count his body, but never once will it take into account the shadows of his absence.

I remember death by its proximity to what I love the most. And the most never looks like freedom, not really. So perfect bow and complete. But the argument of Freedom is not as clean as the driven snow. Not pure. There is blood and history there. Freedom is a container of blood and a living document. It is unanswered question. Remarkable position of positioning. Evergreen in the chase towards its promise. Unchanging coordinates. Accessible to barren land. Prison lacks the imagination. It is the constant undoing of our humanity. Atrophic muscle. Where freedom is a hopeful star. Dream of a memory so close the long whisp of a forgotten breath. Steel bars of unease // consistent qualms // mounting absent. I remember death by its proximity to what I love because incarceration promises everyone it touches: *you will not be the same.* Twenty-two years of prison is an off-balance of a dance towards your humanity. Away from true living. Uncertain chaos. Destruction of filament and family. Life and love are sometimes synonymous, sometimes not. I remember death by its proximity to what I love the most. And the most never looks like freedom, not really. So perfect bow and complete. But the argument of Freedom is not as clean as the driven snow. Not pure. There is blood and history there. Freedom is a container of blood and a living document. It is unanswered question. Remarkable position of positioning. Evergreen in the chase towards its promise. Unchanging coordinates. Accessible to barren land. Prison lacks the imagination. It is the constant undoing of our humanity. Atrophic muscle. Where freedom is a hopeful star. Dream of a memory so close the long whisp of a forgotten breath. Steel bars of unease // consistent qualms // mounting absent. I remember death by its proximity to what I love because incarceration promises everyone it touches: you will not be the same. Twenty-two years of prison is an off-balance of a dance towards your humanity. Away from true living. Uncertain chaos. Destruction of filament and family. Life and love are sometimes synonymous, sometimes not. But death and unliving is no coin toss. Same side of a wooden currency. I remember death is the stone, it lies here and the near here. Therefore, memory is a static image, a missed note forgiven. Memory is the gift of circumstance and the honor of observation. Look at the lightbulb closest to your line of vision. Consider the orb is forgiveness. Reach for the source. Click it dead. Can you still see the illumination of its glow? This is memory in retroaction. It is moving closer and closer to freedom. It is moving closer, this love of. This vibration slides off its coat when you turn in search of the next page. Click it back alive.

Part II

Part II

We don't get how we are all tied to the
prison industrial complex. Nobody's out.

—Mariame Kaba, interviewed by
Mahogany L. Browne, 2019

---

[7] A private prison can offer their services to the government and
     charge $150 per day per prisoner.

Constant

Threat

What is a threat?

Except the possibility of danger
What is dangerous about a black man
beaten for his defiance?

What is defiance except the refusal to bow
the bone that restricts the body from quaking
The threat is all of us

breathing

Constant
Threat

I have nothing else to write about
The steel bars haunt me

I remember death
and it knows my name

We dance a dance
if that is poetic enough

I feel closest to my father
with a dagger in my mouth

Or my mouth is the weapon itself
when I slam bones

Segregated

Like a whisper

Like a promise

If I were a betting woman

I only bet on my ability to slam bones
and walk away from the shaky table, every time
victorious

Segregated

When I play dominoes
I am the one true king
I am the one left breathing

I am
I am
I am
the worst kind of thief
I steal your swag right in front of your own eyes
right in front of your own child

Remember
I'm my father's first daughter

And you will remember my name
It is his, *you know*

And like any horrible tune
radio frequent
with the static
as constant as rain in Orange County[8]
the echo drips:

I am
I am
I am
your king

---

[8] There are thirty-five prisons in California. I miss my father. Since 2017, California's prison population has hovered at about 115,000 inmates. I miss my father. Currently there are 2.2 million people in prison or jail nationwide. I miss my father. California's recidivism rate is ranked among the highest in the country. I miss.

Segregated

Segregated

House 1

I got seven bones[9] & every n/gga at the card table
look like my daddy

---

[9] If you don't know how to play dominoes or the language for it—this
section ain't for you.

House 2

He lose like a body with a heart too soft
He look weak
I bet his demise taste good
I slither
"You ain't been hugged enough" he heard "your mother don't
love you"
His face go slack, my jaws tighten, ready for the blow
The room get ghost
Get silent
Get mosque-like
I praise me today
Watch me become the bed
your mama climb into
every lonely night

House 3

My father been gone a long time
but he taught me don't nobody with any sense
clap for mediocrity
so I don't

The man-child across from me
is a Cheshire grin full of beautiful teeth

He smiles
and I see my father

He laughs
and I see my father

I wonder what it looks like with his blood on my hands
His smile turns into a flatline coast
to the backdrop of no shore
His haunt
be my horizon
Imma rise like the star
Imma rise like Virgin Mary
Imma slam these dominoes
and sip on that brown

wait for his heart to fox-trot from his throat

"Get with it / or get hit with it"

The story arrives
whether or not we are ready
to hold it close

Its little voice singing off-key
with no fear
a kind of truth

The first son of a young man and an even younger woman
lifts like a fist from the red dirt of Homer, Louisiana,
and finds a patch in Berkeley, California,
to toil until it becomes home
Name it the *Big House*

The first son of a father from the military
and a mother with a penchant for horse racing
grows ivy-like from the soil of a Bay Area revolution

First son will forget and then remember the weight
of his hands
will press both thumbs to a human throat
will swing baseball bats in a rage
He will connect with a bag of flesh of bones and dreams

My father
red like the earth from which his parents fled
relocated to a place where eight more would be born
and die

Among the streets of
Berkeley
Oakland
Richmond
Antioch
where each boulevard reeks of blood or car oil
drop-top cherry Chevys burn rubber
An inheritance of abnormal hemoglobin
and a trench of violence
(here violence is considered love, too)

Somewhere in Folsom
a sixty-five-years-aged black man

the eldest of nine siblings
one of the five survivors

is somewhere
His eyes squint until still

hands laced into a steeple
reciting Matthew 5:39[10]

---

[10] But I tell you, do not resist an evil person. If anyone slaps you on the
right cheek, turn to them the other cheek also.

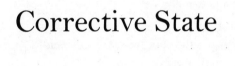

Corrective State

San Quentin ain't got a skyline to dream about
but my uncle's pride in my ability to recover from
an ankle twist on a slab of broken concrete
makes it seem so

They say I play pick-up games
like I've been to the pen
I smirk, a double dribble skipping
across my mistaken face

Twenty years later
a solar system rids a planet
makes itself a new moon
to rock the tides
Still the barbwire and shotguns work like clock
clicks and my father still
doesn't know how many times
I've challenged death

The COVID-19 that spread across my chest
my breathing so close to an island submerged
in fluid // I stuttered awake on the 11th night
I wept until the cold medicine carried me back to sleep
The sickness lie // a boundaryless wretch
It was the most American thing I've ever felt

secure in my home and still dying from the heat
of capitalism

They are reopening the world after the planet
tried to reset itself

And the prisons are still packed with people
afraid to believe in redemption
Racist-adjacent smiles
forgive white collar crimes
as hedge funds funnel into
protective custody / a static of dispatch
The walls clean with other men's teeth

Antibody tests smell like Henrietta Lacks
coming back to remind us of what happens
when you trust a house of poachers

They call us ungovernable

The way we picket and protest
this mourning / is a reminder
steel bars don't melt with silence

The people behind bars are captives of war
The people behind bars are captives of war
The people stolen into camps and cages
stretch beyond the steel
An unshakeable whisper tremors our collectivity

I want to go home
I want to hold my daughter
I want to see my mother one last time

There ain't no poem in that

The human form was not meant to be locked up //

locked down / cage bound // consider your own

bones /// the way you lengthen as soon as you turn

your face to the sun /// a mask over your nose //

relinquish yourself to this adaptation of love /// and

inhale the day // crisp in its welcome

Send a kite to Folsom
as we correct our form

Acknowledgments

For my mama. Thank you for loving, raising, and lifting me the best way you knew how.

My gratitude to Rauschenberg Residency, Art for Justice Fund, Oakland, California, Tiffany Faye, Charlotte Sheedy Literary Agency, Cornelius Eady, Ross Gay, Maya Marshall, Ocean Vuong, Jive Poetic, Tongo Eisen-Martin. Because of your guidance, time, and friendship, I was able to write my way home.

Resources

Bureau of Statistics

The Business Model of Private Prisons | Investopedia

California Innocence Project

Crime Report from John Jay College

Fragile Families and Child Wellbeing Study

Inside the World's Toughest Prisons

Orange County Register

Key to Acronyms

ASP—Avenal State Prison

CAC—California City Correctional Facility

CCC—California Correctional Center

CCI—California Correctional Institution

CHCF—California Health Care Facility

CIM— California Institution for Men

CIW—California Institution for Women

CMF—California Medical Facility

CMC—California Men's Colony

CRC—California Rehabilitation Center

CEN—California State Prison, Centinela

COR—California State Prison, Corcoran

LAC—California State Prison, Los Angeles County

SAC—California State Prison, Sacramento

SOL—California State Prison, Solano

SATF—California Substance Abuse Treatment Facility and State Prison, Corcoran

CAL—Calipatria State Prison

CCWF—Central California Women's Facility

CVSP—Chuckawalla Valley State Prison

CTF—Correctional Training Facility

DVI—Deuel Vocational Institution

FSP—Folsom State Prison

HDSP—High Desert State Prison

ISP—Ironwood State Prison

KVSP—Kern Valley State Prison

MCSP—Mule Creek State Prison

NKSP—North Kern State Prison

PBSP—Pelican Bay State Prison

PVSP—Pleasant Valley State Prison

RJD—Richard J. Donovan Correctional Facility

SVSP—Salinas Valley State Prison

SQ—San Quentin State Prison

SCC—Sierra Conservation Center

VSPW—Valley State Prison for Women

WSP—Wasco State Prison

About the Author

Mahogany L. Browne is the Executive Director of JustMedia, a media literacy initiative designed to support the groundwork of criminal justice leaders and community members. This position is informed by her career as a writer, organizer, and educator. Browne has received fellowships from Agnes Gund, Air Serenbe, Cave Canem, Poets House, Mellon Foundation, and Rauschenberg Foundation. Browne is the author of recent works: *Chlorine Sky, Woke: A Young Poets Call to Justice, Woke Baby,* and *Black Girl Magic.* She is also the founder of the diverse lit initiative, the Woke Baby Book Fair. *I Remember Death By Its Proximity to What I Love* is her thirteenth collection of poems. She lives in Brooklyn, New York.

About Haymarket Books

Haymarket Books is a radical, independent, nonprofit book publisher based in Chicago. Our mission is to publish books that contribute to struggles for social and economic justice. We strive to make our books a vibrant and organic part of social movements and the education and development of a critical, engaged, international left.

We take inspiration and courage from our namesakes, the Haymarket martyrs, who gave their lives fighting for a better world. Their 1886 struggle for the eight-hour day—which gave us May Day, the international workers' holiday—reminds workers around the world that ordinary people can organize and struggle for their own liberation. These struggles continue today across the globe—struggles against oppression, exploitation, poverty, and war.

Since our founding in 2001, Haymarket Books has published more than five hundred titles. Radically independent, we seek to drive a wedge into the risk-averse world of corporate book publishing. Our authors include Noam Chomsky, Arundhati Roy, Rebecca Solnit, Angela Y. Davis, Howard Zinn, Amy Goodman, Wallace Shawn, Mike Davis, Winona LaDuke, Ilan Pappé, Richard Wolff, Dave Zirin, Keeanga-Yamahtta Taylor, Nick Turse, Dahr Jamail, David Barsamian, Elizabeth Laird, Amira Hass, Mark Steel, Avi Lewis, Naomi Klein, and Neil Davidson. We are also the trade publishers of the acclaimed Historical Materialism Book Series and of Dispatch Books.

Also Available from Haymarket Books

1919 | by Eve L. Ewing

Black Girl Magic | edited by Mahogany L. Browne, Idrissa Simmonds, and Jamila Woods, foreword by Patricia Smith

Bloodstone Cowboy | by Kara Jackson

Build Yourself a Boat | by Camonghne Felix

Can I Kick It? | by Idris Goodwin

Crossfire: A Litany for Survival | by Staceyann Chin, foreword by Jacqueline Woodson

Doppelgangbanger | by Cortney Lamar Charleston

Halal If You Hear Me | edited by Fatimah Asghar and Safia Elhillo

If God Is a Virus | by Seema Yasmin

LatiNext | Edited by Felicia Chavez, José Olivarez, and Willie Perdomo

Lineage of Rain | by Janel Pinéda

Mama Phife Represents: A Memoir | by Cheryl Boyce-Taylor

Milagro | by Penelope Alegria

Too Much Midnight | by Krista Franklin